Postcards from Paradise

Poems
by
Jennifer Lagier

Blue Light Press ❖ 1st World Publishing

San Francisco ❖ Fairfield ❖ Delhi

Postcards from Paradise
Copyright ©2023 by Jennifer Lagier

All rights reserved. Printed in the United States of America. No part of this book may be used or reproduced in any manner whatsoever without written permission except in the case of brief quotations embodied in critical articles and reviews. For information contact:

1st World Library
PO Box 2211
Fairfield, IA 52556
www.1stworldpublishing.com

Blue Light Press
www.bluelightpress.com
bluelightpress@aol.com

Book & Cover Design
Melanie Gendron
melaniegendron999@gmail.com

Cover Art
Gene McCormick

Author Photo
Oliver Fellguth

First Edition

Library of Congress Cataloging-in-Publication Data

ISBN: 978-1-4218-3548-8

Praise for *Postcards from Paradise*

"Jennifer Lagier's *Postcards from Paradise* is a poet's travelogue that is deeply engaged with the places she is visiting. A Rhine River cruise yields poems of Amsterdam, Vienna and Paris among other highlights. A longer, extended sequence reveals deeper connection with Spain that expresses both the beauty and harsher realities of life there. However, it is time spent in Hawaii, a place she knows and loves, that reveals her gift for describing the natural world. Here, in an earthly paradise, she celebrates her wedding anniversary on the Day of the Dead. What could be more romantic than that?"

– Alan Catlin, poet and editor, *Misfit Magazine*

"*Postcards From Paradise* is a collection of travel poems that assumes we are in the poet's pocket as she views the scenery through a poet's lens. Holocaust memorials and the bicycles of Europe nudge against the fervor of Alicante and the majesty of the Swiss Alps. Poems place you in the scene and tug, as if you were sitting with the poet drinking coffee in a café discussing the evening's sunset. The old and new combine from "unhealed battle wounds" to standing where Martin Luther once stood and "ancient German Kings mingle with the Apple Store." In France, Heloise's powerful words combine with "a symphony of tiny sparrows lifting." Nature is front and center in the Hawaii poems where "palm trees battered by rain perform a frenzied hula." She ends the book with mystical travel in Mayan country where "cameras and tourists capture only hints of an overthrown culture." What Jennifer Lagier depicts in this book brings to life what only an observant poet can capture for readers interested in broader horizons. This is a must read for anyone who wants to open their panorama and take a journey with great poems from great locations."

– Lisha Adela García, author of *Blood Rivers* and *A Rope of Luna*

"Jennifer Lagier's poetry lights the passage to a larger world of global citizenship. She shows us how to venture out and find beauty and connection in small corners of the human present – mimes at Sacre-Coeur, posters of street boys in a Paris wine shop, bicycles in Amsterdam, barges on the Rhine, astronomical clocks, fountains, tombs of housewives and writers. This book describes the passionate journey of a woman wanting to *see*, not just *know about*, the world. And she takes us with her through lush lyricism of a hungry eye and an open heart. Jennifer captures the magic and energy of spaces where rivers like the Rhine and Moselle meet, expressing it all in poems, which she calls postcards, rich in insight, description, humor and care for the places she visits."

– Mary Kay Rummel, poet laureate emerita of Ventura County, CA

"What an immense pleasure to stow away on Jennifer Lagier's grand poetic vessel *Postcards from Paradise*. In her newest published volume, Jenn "swills poetry" like the sangria flowing through one of her verses from Spain. By turns playful and profound, she bids us to enter as "poetry knocks on (her) soul's door" as she writes her way through delightful destinations in Switzerland, Spain, Hawaii and France."

"In "Rooster Reveille," we wake with her to a "love-sick Nene goose's crooning complaint." Ghosts of literary and musical icons rear up, spewing life hacks, as our poet wends her way through Paris' famed Pere Lachaise cemetery. Or, one can almost sense that voyeur blackbird's fixed, beady eyes on her sidestroking form in a Mexican hotel's tepid pool. Finally, reading "Carne" *nearly* convinced me to ignore longtime vegetarian leanings and succumb to all those meat-loving countries' mouth-watering offerings."

"Even if, like me, the pandemic limited *your* travels to a twenty mile radius, wrap your fanciful mind and heart around Jennifer Lagier's *Postcards from Paradise*! Let it transport you to a world "serene in lavender moments" where the "Yucatan sun bakes away every worry."

– Barbara Saxton, author of *Dual Exposure* and contributor to various poetry anthologies and publications

"Traveling – it leaves you speechless, then turns you into a storyteller."
– Ibn Battuta

Contents

Amsterdam Bicycles 1
Electric Ladyland: The First Museum of Fluorescent Art 2
Kinderdijk Windmills 3
Koblenz Keepsakes 4
Speyer, Germany 6
Cologne Misadventure 7
Going Medieval in Colmar 9
Strasbourg Soaking 10
Artifacts 11
Lucerne 12
Exploring Lucerne 13
Interlaken 14
Paris at Midnight 16
Pere Lachaise 17
Love Among Ruin 18
Heloise's Epistle 19
Bronze Stud 20
Notre Dame Symphony 21
Montmartre Adventure 22
Cabaret after Sunrise 23
Persistent Memory 24
Visiting Versailles 25
Strike 26
Expatriate 27
Alicante 28
Elche 29
Carne 30
Madrid 31
Mimo 32
Negra y Angel 33
Beach Esplanade 34
Tapas y Tequila 35

Emigrada	36
Pim Pam Pollo	37
Rainstorm	38
Autumn on Kauai	39
Princeville Sunrise	40
Trade Winds	41
Pele's Delinquents	42
Halloween on Kauai	43
Hanalei Halloween	44
Tahiti Nui	45
Bubba Burgers	46
Molten	47
Rooster Reveille	48
After Deluge	49
From Westin to St. Regis	50
Princeville Meander	51
Hanalei Overlook	52
Kauai Rain	53
Taro	54
Calavera for Kauai	55
Tree Tunnel	56
Approaching the Day of the Dead	57
Hanalei Bay Resort	58
Plumeria	59
Sunset on Kauai	60
Cancun	61
Tulum (2018)	62
Iguana	63
Macaws	64
Lifeguard	65
Yucatan Menage	66
Isla Mujeres	67
Tulum (2012)	68
Acknowledgements	71
About the Author	73

Amsterdam Bicycles

Our cruise guide cites statistics:
nearly 1 million bicycles in Amsterdam,
15,000 pulled from canals each year.
We immediately learn to avoid
red bike paths, pedaling commuters,
flinch at the sound of dinging bells,
jump curbs to avoid lethal collisions.

Bicycles congregate at Central Station,
near schools, museums, restaurants,
line streets along rows of tall, brick apartments.
Riders haul children, groceries, entire families
all over town in black bin attachments.
Along Stadhouderskade near our hotel,
we observe one man balancing white filing cabinet
atop fork-mounted milk crate.

Senior citizens, kids, men, and women
whizz past our cautious pedestrian forays
down skinny cobblestone sidewalks.
While we cringe and hug store fronts,
French bulldogs, Pomeranians, Pugs
joyfully travel in handlebar baskets.

Electric Ladyland:
The First Museum of Fluorescent Art

It's like revisiting my 1968 bedroom:
Jimi Hendrix posters on every wall,
Escher prints, black lights,
psychedelic sculptures and colors.

Our curator is an expatriate burnout,
no stranger to LSD, hash, possibly heroin.
Heat pulses from orange dayglo walls.
A chubby tabby cat purrs from paisley bench.
Ancient spider plants dangle
between strands of macramaed hemp holders.

I descend steep stairwell sans handrail,
nothing more than a dangerous ladder.
In the humid depths, pressed against
fourteen sweaty, twenty-something strangers,
asthma blossoms as I struggle for breath.

Claustrophobia overcomes.
I pull myself up wooden step rungs.
From below, familiar riffs of
Hey Joe, Are You Experienced,
then an electrified, acid-fueled version
of the *Star-Spangled Banner.*

Kinderdijk Windmills

We board a hundred-year-old barge
purchased by UNESCO for a single euro,
motor down a south Holland canal
shaped by Rhine Delta waters.
18th century windmills tower over levees
along a patchwork of fields
amid reclaimed farmland, low-lying polders.
Tan and white cattle munch reeds
among apple trees, sunflowers.

A millwright with wooden shoes
clumps out to meet us,
demonstrates how to unfurl canvas sails
to catch and harness wind,
stomps upon spoked wheel
to winch rotored mill head
in the proper direction.

For generations, families handed down
their special craft, father to son,
pumping rainwater from pasture
to canal, Rhine River channel,
back into North Sea.
A tall stake painted with red, yellow,
black slash lines demark
historical levels of flooding.

We're soft American tourists,
intimidated by claustrophobic built-in bed,
little floor space, cramped outdoor kitchen,
a way of life alien to first-world privilege
on display, preserved by museum.

Koblenz Keepsakes

"The ancient Romans once christened the city Confluentes, a name derived from the city's location at the confluence of the Rhine and Moselle rivers."
– Funky Germany: The Travel Site

The Fortress of Ehrenbreitstein towers above us.
Built in the tenth century, destroyed, then reconstructed,
legend claims it once contained the tunic Christ wore
just before crucifixion.

On command, our group gathers in a grassy Koblenz Park
at the intersection of Rhine and Moselle Rivers.
We admire Roman ruins, visit a Kaiser Wilhelm I statue.

The towering bronze emperor gazes toward Germany.
His horse has been strategically positioned,
ass facing France, a political statement
in response to repeated French occupation.

Our tour guide is an amateur comic,
tells us parking tickets
are the most common Koblenz souvenirs.
The German Department of Order
has no patience with motorists who ignore signs
screaming VERBOTEN.

We visit Gorresplatz Square
with its fountain of a spitting schoolboy,
loiter before a carved statue of the Virgin Mary
cradling an orb-clutching baby Jesus and a gold scepter.
Annoyed locals plough through invading visitors,
demand we step aside as they hurry
to cathedrals, bookshops, cafes.

Several of us mutiny, find a coffee shop,
take a time out, snap photos, nibble pastry,
sip frothy lattes, steaming espresso.

Speyer, Germany

Our tour guide lists what's wrong
with Speyer public schools,
identifies Old Town Gate, medieval synagogue ruins,
explains local customs.

If a woman isn't married by age 31,
town folks bake a bread mate
to compensate for absent husband,
parade life-sized pastry down cobblestone streets
to a mock ceremony before the church altar.

An aging bride clutches her bouquet of orange flowers,
waits for family and groom outside city hall.
The guide confesses she proposed
to her long-time, marriage-shy boyfriend,
became a wife just before that terminal birthday.
Divorced after one child, now she is bitter.

We view a towering statue of Martin Luther.
I stand where he once defied the pope,
questioned doctrine, demanded religious reform.
Later, we pass golden cobbles before houses
in the Jewish quarter inscribed
with names of local Holocaust victims.

Cathedrals, tombs of Holy Roman emperors,
ancient German Kings mingle with Apple store,
McDonalds, sportswear boutiques.
We commandeer a café table,
imbibe from glass jars filled with coffee, vanilla ice cream.
Centuries of history leave me exhausted.

Cologne Misadventure

> *"Cologne's Old Town has a distinctive historical charm. Visitors are drawn by its rustic narrow alleyways lined with traditional old houses. Innumerable breweries, pubs and restaurants invite passersby to linger."*
> – www.cologne-tourism.com

All night we cruise down the Rhine,
navigate sixteen concrete locks,
grateful recent rains have raised water levels
enough for safe passage.

In the morning, we anchor in Cologne,
take a shuttle bus to downtown,
pass through a gauntlet of carved saints,
pause beneath Gothic arch,
admire stained-glass windows
depicting stations of the cross,
regal insignia, a heart spilling flames.

Later, we meet a tattooed cousin,
his pierced and inked girlfriend,
practice shaky German, marginal English
over lunch, followed by coffee,
bowls of plum and berry gelato.

At the chocolate museum,
we take advantage of free public restrooms,
sniff overpowering cocoa scent,
accept handfuls of foil-wrapped candy.
They hug us, climb into their car
for a four-hour drive home to Hamburg.

Spurning transport back to our ship,
we wander through a botanical garden,
purchase bottles of water
from a closet-sized grocery.

A riverbank trail meanders
past white townhouses with red geraniums,
along a fenced shipyard
under bejeweled blanket of berries.

Ten and a half miles later, we reach the pier,
just before the captain's six-p.m. curfew,
return to our cabin for a much-needed shower.

Going Medieval in Colmar

French countryside displays unhealed battle wounds,
medieval fences and moats, bombed ruins of castles.
Our guide points out the site where Audie Murphy
took on a German tank, defeated Nazi aggressors.

Old town's pink and blue half-timbered,
early renaissance buildings line water-lilied canals.
Red geraniums tumble from window boxes as tiny skiffs
drop passengers at cafes, private piers.

Hundreds of scarlet padlocks
fastened to wrought iron bridge railings
signify visitors who arrived, fell in love,
took root within shuttered apartments.

Above shops selling linen, foie gras, sausages,
wooden effigies of storks, geese, or sows dangle.
Street vendors hawk tee shirts, gelato, pastries.
My husband photographs me
beside a multicolored ceramic giraffe.

Against rocky Alsatian hillsides,
rows of crucified grapevines.
Autumn rain spatters slippery cobbles.
In La Petite Venice, we find an empty table,
nibble buttery croissant, sip steamy latte.

Strasbourg Soaking

Lavender rain cloudscape herringbones charcoal sky.
We shuttle past the International Institute of Human Rights,
cross from Germany into France
over a steel trellis bridge transecting the Rhine.

Moss-green canals mirror Romanesque buildings
housing bakeries, coffee shops, restaurants.
Gothic cathedral spires pierce nimbostratus clouds.
Swan flotillas navigate between sightseeing gondolas.

Slick cobblestones, a string of bicyclists,
skinny streets lead us to Notre Dame.
We are dazzled by stained glass pentacles,
14th century astronomical clock,
Death chasing the devil,
a procession of Christ and his apostles
summoned by mechanical rooster.

Later, we are caught in an unending deluge,
unsuccessfully seek shelter beneath golden sycamores,
cower within a stone arch above flooded stairwell.
Gutters fill, overflow, turn passageways into rivers.
Sodden, we press together for warmth
under borrowed umbrella.

Artifacts

On either side of the Rhine River,
perched among scarlet foliage,
roofless ruins of cathedrals,
stucco wineries, medieval stone castles.

Ziplines stitch together a succession of hilltops.
Along hidden tracks, a silver train speeds
above clusters of bikes bearing pedaling tourists.

Despite global warming, critically low water level,
our ship cruises from Amsterdam to Basel
escorted by power boats, turgid barges,
one brave canoeist.

At each port, I sample regional delicacies,
become addicted to ice cream,
pastries, potatoes, and pork,
lard on surplus pounds.

Lucerne

As we enter Switzerland
I began craving cheese,
think of my grandfather,
born just northwest of Luzern
beside Lake Maggiore,
spiritually return to family roots,
never felt more Swiss-Italian.

Light rain and bitter cold
flow with Alpine mist
from steep, forested mountains.
Slippery cobblestone streets
transect clusters of ancient churches,
old mansions converted into hotels,
restaurants, boutiques.
We wander a sycamore-lined path
that circles ebony lake fed
by melting glaciers.

In our spare suite
created from a sixteenth century castle,
I reel from jetlag, rich food,
a surfeit of caffeinated espresso,
find myself missing Monterey,
our little dogs, my old home,
fragrant xeriscape garden.

Exploring Lucerne

Shuttling from cruise ship to Lucerne,
we pass through jagged mountains, spruce forests,
valleys speckled with chateaus, turquoise lakes,
pastures crowded with milk cows.

Stopping at the Lion Monument,
we shiver, brave icy rain to snap photos
of a wounded beast rendered in marble,
take advantage of free public restrooms.

The bus driver drops us at the railway station
a block from hotel room overlooking outdoor market.
Before us spreads navy blue Lake Luzern,
a customary stop on European Grand Tours.

We stroll along the Reuss River,
photograph stone water tower,
wooden Chapel Bridge decorated
with 17th-century paintings.

In Old Town, a mural depicts water mills.
Tourists clutter walkway, outdoor tables,
congregate along marble stairway
ascending from waterway to baroque Jesuit Church.

A whimsical statue of a Swiss boy
grinning face with Pinocchio nose,
clad in lederhosen, traditional vest, slip on shoes,
waves the Swiss flag.

Interlaken

> *By the beginning of the 19th century Interlaken in the Bernese Oberland had already become renowned for its impressive mountain scenery. Famous contemporaries such as Johann Wolfgang von Goethe and Felix Mendelssohn traveled in these mountains.*
> *– myswitzerland.com*

On our final day in Lucerne,
we board Die Zentralbahn train,
begin our trip to an ancient Alpine resort.

Climbing, we pass five crystalline lakes,
vertical rock faces, looping hiking trails,
small villages with pointy church steeples.

Just before Brünig Pass, cogwheel technology
kicks in to conquer steep gradient,
pulls us past waterfalls, remnants of glaciers.

Their glory days long gone,
faded Interlaken hotels and chalets appear,
give way to flowery town square.

We browse tourist traps filled
with chocolate bars, Swiss Army knives,
tour guides, assorted trinkets.

I purchase throat lozenges,
Coke Zero, a mediocre panini.
We settle into our seats, begin the descent.

Emerald meadows revive family stories,
remembrances of reading Heidi,
scenes from The Sound of Music.

We muse about Swiss simplicity,
high-altitude isolation,
research immigration.

Paris at Midnight

Along the Seine, three empty pill vials,
abandoned brassiere, twisted violet thong.

Passing bateaux trail laughter, cheers,
rough trade taxi dance music.

Book sellers and bistros line shadowy left bank,
colorful backdrops for romantic drama.

Silver fountains pulse and arouse.
Lovers embrace, silhouetted by moonlight.

Pere Lachaise

Our guide, Jean-Jacques, divulges
seedy political and sexual scandals
behind bland inscriptions
carved upon marble mausoleums.

We pass grandiose tombs within which
angels and antichrists decompose
beside housewives and saints.
Effigies of the Buchenwald slaughtered
are resurrected in bronze,
hold hands and dance.

Fading lipstick kisses polka dot
Oscar Wilde's neutered sphinx.
According to rumor,
a bureaucrat anchors paperwork
with the severed stone sex.

Gertrude Stein holds her final soiree
among Balzac, Colette, deceased literati.
Jim Morrison's bronze bust has been stolen,
a single red poppy, twist of marijuana
left in its place.

Love Among Ruin

"The more stubbornly it persisted, the more fiercely we believed." – Louise Gluck

Among quiet mausoleums, still lovers
are caught leaning forward to kiss.

The man's stone hands lovingly cup
the graceful oval of his wife's marble face.

He caresses her cheekbones, enthralled
despite the closed door of death.

She stares adoringly into his blind eyes,
a monument of frozen constancy.

I am a curious tourist, pausing to
wistfully ponder their eternal embrace.

Heloise's Epistle
After visiting their tomb at Pere Lachaise

Beloved, heal the wounds
you have inflicted. Remember,
I was the one who refused to lie,
rejected wedlock for freedom.

Destroyed myself at your command,
changed open doors for sealed convent
simply to prove you the sole possessor
of my heart, soul, and will.

You who lavish time
on proud disbelievers,
consider your growing debt
to the neglected faithful.

My broken spirit is a weak plantation
sown with tender, ailing plants
that require nourishing sun,
your careful attention.

Treachery robbed me of myself
in robbing me of you.
I fear nothing more than barren silence,
this claustrophobic sentence I am now serving.

Only letters provide a lingering hint
of your long-absent presence,
vague words that still caress,
despite the malice of others.

Bronze Stud

All I've ever learned from love was how to shoot somebody who outdrew you
– Leonard Cohen

It's a certainty you made demoiselles swoon
with your brash, rogue demeanor.

I know your type—too quick-witted for your own good,
lacking sense to evade insulted avengers.

You excelled at wounding with words,
wicked ink striking deep from innocent cover.

This time, your cornered prey drew his own loaded weapon.
Even beyond the grave, your bronzed body swaggers.

The lonely and barren come after darkness,
caress your permanently turned cheek.

Mute muse of the erotically forlorn,
red carnations and adoration can't warm you.

Notre Dame Symphony

Inside a husk of stone, voices
of the martyred rattle like seeds.

Gargoyles snatch passing souls.
Gothic spires erupt from colorless slate.

Medieval clerics shattered intricate
stained glass, always hungry for light.

In the courtyard, a man raises one arm,
blesses tourists, conducts his own mass.

A symphony of tiny sparrows lift,
flutter skyward bearing sinners' requests.

Montmartre Adventure

I evade prepubescent
pickpockets who stalk naive
tourists as they emerge from
the underground Metro.

A watchful Parisian wordlessly
points from his eyes to my wallet,
warns of gypsy hands that grab,
distracting their victims.

Eight blocks later, gendarmes
apprehend the young thieves,
force them to sit in a line,
wrists bound, feet in the gutter.

Sketch artists, white-faced mimes,
solicit at Sacre-Coeur cathedral,
posture, entertain passersby,
make indecent proposals to women.

Near the Lapin Agile Cabaret,
I visit a wine shop, walls illustrated
with street boys, the French
equivalent of Salinas gang homies.

A late afternoon Crocque Monseiur,
warm beer mixed with lemonade,
kicking back at an open air bistro,
make me fit in, feel like a local.

Cabaret after Sunrise

Once the Moulin Rouge closes, tourists are
sent back to five-star hotels, accounts settled,
indiscretions forgiven, slumming concluded.

Seductive courtesans call it a night, wander
home to single beds, feed the cat,
set out tea and biscuits, decide to sleep in.

Daylight scrubs away most erotic adventures.
Young dancers wash their faces, cover up
flawless breasts, pull on faded levis.

Red windmill rotor blades whirl.
A fresh shift of Montmarte pickpockets
spill from the Metro.

Persistent Memory

Inside Monet's house, copper pans against
blue wallpaper, vivid floral canvas vignettes.
Artists stroll along midnight boulevards,
inhabit Parisian kitchens, Bohemian salons.

Outside, beneath a weeping willow,
his green rowboat swings in the wind.
Watercolors immortalize shadows,
gravel shores, creaking vacancy.

Overlapping lily pads float upon
shimmering pond, refract wavy
impressions of wisteria, Japanese bridge,
feathery clumps of golden bamboo.

Painters set up easels, canvas,
create persistent memories
of inverted pink roses, liquid
delphinium, reflected azaleas.

Visiting Versailles

This is opulence on a scale that staggers,
in-your-face ostentation, oblivious privilege.

Gold leaf encrusts fantastical murals, carved ceilings
where crystal chandeliers blaze, illuminate hallways.

Mirrors, tapestries, priceless art transform grand apartments
into vivid galleries of inflated heroism within a lifeless museum.

Marble statues tower over courtiers, royalty, servants,
turn a blind eye to indiscretions, overlook peccadillos.

Each supersized room is cluttered with glittering treasures.
Windows far from revolutionary rabble frame formal gardens.

Strike

200,000 workers,
furious at the government's proposal
to raise retirement age by two years,
take to Parisian streets,
close down the Metro,
restaurants, museums,
chant slogans, carry
red balloons, colorful banners.

At night, they riot along
Avenue des Champs-Élysées,
light fires in trash cans,
toss rocks and bottles.

I escape my Marais district hotel,
drop into the local bistro,
knock back a few glasses
of lukewarm *panaché*,
feel union sympathies stirring.

After three or four,
I'm out on the boulevard
waving a scarlet flag
and pumping one fist
with my new anarchist friends,
an expatriate American lefty,
inebriated and incensed.

I march in solidarity
among rowdy French strikers.

Expatriate

I breeze through security,
unpack laptop, check email,
Facebook, from an airport café.
The trim waiter brings hot chowder,
an icy mimosa, offers tempting desserts.

In an hour, I'll lift off from San Francisco,
wave goodbye to parched California:
crowded cookie cutter houses,
empty reservoirs,
snowless Sierras.

At the boarding gate,
I can finally relax,
imagine a clean slate,
reinvented reality,
starting over elsewhere.

Departure from Been There and Done it to Death.
Destination: Adventure. Possibility. Barcelona. Madrid.

Alicante

I wander wonderland byways:
dizzying Paseo de la Explanada de España,
secret plazas, their kiosks and fountains,
skinny alley decorated with fantastical mushrooms.
I discover tiny cafes serving pizza and tapas.
Treat myself to Spanish beer, then flan
complimented by cups of espresso.
Return the smile of a dark Spaniard who winks,
generously foots the bill for my sangria.
Watch beautiful men holding hands,
sipping champagne at a yacht harbor bistro.
Spend the night in a penthouse overlooking
high rise apartments, twitching ocean,
flickering streetlights.
Welcome steamy sunrise
from between satin sheets.

Elche

Modern strip malls and offices
surround palm trees, fountain, municipal park.
Everywhere, antique sculpture and art.
Picturesque plazas offer cafes and cantinas,
al fresco dining where fragrant tapas seduce.

Red, gold, and sapphire paint
transform arid aqueduct into vivid mural.
A stone basilica shares the square
with gelato stand, farmacia,
La Biblioteca saloon.

I devour fried cheese,
blood sausage with scrambled eggs,
drink sangria among old books until 10 p.m.
Celebrate new friends, fresh perspective.
Savor a pulsing night on the town.

Carne

While in Spain, I renounce
my vegetarian past, crave meat
in every manifestation, morning and night.
Salivate over salami, thin prosciutto slices,
grow wet at the sight of foil-wrapped ham.

Crisp bacon seduces,
weans me from breakfast yogurt.
Siren song of steak and sangria for lunch.
By dinner, my appetite is reduced
to bruschetta sprinkled with chorizo,
a bit of green salad, shards of hard cheese.

All night I fantasize flesh in many forms:
succulent pork, mouth-watering beef.
Sleep soundly, lost in carnal dreams.

Madrid

I salute policia wearing blue uniforms, twirling threatening guns.
They form a mandatory reception line leading into the train terminal
where I am divested of purse and belt, subjected to a full body scan.

In the coach car, passengers sit, two by two.
An attendant pushes a squeaky cart down the narrow aisle,
dispenses espresso, newspapers, travel advice.

Green fields, leafless vineyards, graffitied concrete flash by.
A gravel-voiced matron shouts "Hola!" conducts
impassioned conversations at high decibel
throughout the trip on her over-sized phone.

In Madrid, civil guardsman, chunky vans on every corner.
Mimes and street performers command crammed plazas,
banter with tourists, beg for attention, coins, applause.

Crowds surround cathedrals, museums,
the Prada where young soldiers swarm.
I move from bistro to café,
finally an umbrella table beside park kiosk,
sip sparkling wine among pink blossoming trees
in a demilitarized zone.

Mimo

I have known my share of chameleons.
This silver Spaniard with metallic stage props
simply one more performance artist
camouflaged by imaginative makeup.
He postures, plays to the crowd,
donation can before his podium,
aggressively shilling for money.

The man has neither humility nor shame.
Stares and smirks, intuits exactly
what I am thinking
as I fling a small coin,
pause to appraise
his trim, muscular body.

Negra y Angel

A dark angel leads me
past my comfort zone
through a canyon of high-rise apartments,
along cracked, slanting sidewalks,
on her way to antique city center,
then to the sea.

Around me, spray painted gang slogans,
intricate graffiti artwork.
Children wave paper streamers on sticks.
Elderly men and women pull shopping carts
or hold leashes tethered to small, ratty dogs.

Outside each tienda,
black stockinged shop girls cluster,
clutch lit cigarettes,
gesture and share juicy gossip,
howl with laughter,
blow blue smoke into brisk breeze.

Beach Esplanade

I explore the old town beach promenade.
Dizzying bands of cream, green and rust tiles wriggle
between inns, marketplace booths, white swath of sand.
Before 10 a.m., a thin stream of curious tourists.
Here and there, an elderly couple walking their dog.

I marvel at pastel high-rise apartments,
their wrought iron balconies floating gardens
of scarlet geranium, vivid nasturtium,
imagine what it must look like at night,
boisterous crowds traversing patterned path,
waving ever-present cigarettes, clutching cold beers.

From my café table abutting the esplanade,
I sip potent espresso, watch joggers,
a shirtless roller blader with muscular legs,
sigh at the sight of his rippling abs.

Tapas y Tequila

I stumble into the midst of a church procession,
allergic to piety, crave an antidote to religion.
Head to Plaza Santa Barbara and my favorite café.
Order tapas and tequila, discretely settle into a nook,
eavesdrop on couples canoodling at dark corner tables.

Bartender Luis knows my weaknesses, serves local scandal
in lisping Spanish over espresso, sangria.
Chalks today's paella specials on blackboards
hung from ancient stone walls at the foot of a staircase.
Croons sexily with music videos, holds out a hand,
invites me to join him.

"When in Spain," I think, knocking back a shot.
Grind my way to the dance floor.

Emigrada

I consider renouncing American citizenship,
relocation to a funky Alicante flat
overlooking cafes and pocket parks,
glimpse of silvery ocean.

I imagine morning excursions
tethered to the leash of a fat, spoiled Chihuahua,
casual flirtation with lively gentlemen
still in possession of that certain sparkle.

Mine would be the wrought iron balcony
spilling red geraniums, after-dark laughter.
Envision intimacy on my terrace sipping wine
beside the evening's hot lover.

Pim Pam Pollo

Lard is a sacrament dispensed at this Spanish food booth:
dismembered chicken, flayed potato fragments crisped
in a baptismal vat of molten, roiling fat.

The graffiti advertisement of a wok is very deceptive,
implies healthy stir-fry, succulent veggies,
wishful thinking, wildly imaginative street art.

I watch patrons crunch fried nuggets
from cardboard containers, wipe greasy hands
on brown paper napkins as their arteries harden.

Rainstorm

As I dejectedly pack my suitcase,
the Alicante skies open, wash ancient buildings
and congested streets with silver downpour.
Thunder grumbles, wallops rain from storm clouds,
matches conflicting emotions, dark mood.

The last day in Spain and there's still
so many unexplored cantinas,
but my return flight to California
lifts off just after dawn.

Pink trees shower wet streets
with wind propelled blossoms.
I dig out passport, break down computer.

This time tomorrow, I'll clear customs in Madrid,
then again in Chicago, suffer re-entry jet lag,
sleep overnight, if I can, in San Francisco.

I review poem drafts on my hard drive,
text friends back on the Monterey Peninsula,
wonder when I'll be able to wander again.

Autumn on Kauai

"with such cheer as even the leaf must wear as it unfurls its fragrant body..."
– Mary Oliver

Pele's feisty roosters screech,
challenge the audacity of daybreak,
chase pompous Nenes and timid doves.
Their crowing grates nerves, penetrates sleep.

Rising sun sizzles against palms, pines, hibiscus.
Blushing rain clouds float above scarlet ti trees,
monster philodendron, banana leaf jungle.
Swollen cumulus billow, suffused with tropical colors.

Blustery blue storms sweep ashore,
dump warm silver payload.
Battered plumeria revert to bare limbs,
autumn reflected in an absence of flowers.

Transported from arid California shores,
even the most austere succumb
to sensual saturation, perfumed head winds.
Brilliant, broken gardens let the soul blossom.

Princeville Sunrise

I wake to a love-sick Nene goose's crooning complaint.
Pele's consort joins the cacophony, screeching herald of sunrise.

Palm fronds rattle, ripple in rising wind.
Pinkish thunderheads threaten silvery downpour.

I hike the north shore, admire emerald Bali Hai,
wave propelled spindrift creaming on coral.

At poolside, children decorate pumpkins with magic markers.
Randy adults sip mimosas, nuzzle in grottoes.

Tonight, All Hallows Eve, restless spirits and zombies.
I sit before nightly news on a flat screen TV, watch scary movies.

Trade Winds

Island roosters are agitated, pace damp lawn,
crow off-key, feel a change in the weather.

With first light, breezes pick up,
dance with plumeria, hibiscus,
push livid thunderheads inland.

Avocado trees are unwillingly singing.
Sea birds chirp, spread the news,
a monsoon is coming.

Trade winds are all the buzz.
Doves and nervous chickens
go into hiding.

I wake to the rattle of palm fronds,
silver spatter of downpour.

Pele's Delinquents

In olden times on Kauai,
colorful roosters were sacrificed
to placate fire goddess, Pele.

Slashed, dripping blood from red
and bronze plumage, they were tribute
to appease volcanos, halt burning lava.

This morning a frisky descendant
harries hens, annoys Nene geese,
crows and wakes up the tourists.

Full of himself, he struts
around the swimming pool,
pecks at my flip flops.

Later, he gathers
his thuggish gang
for afternoon deployment.

Like a miniature band
of arrogant brown shirts,
they bully and berate.

Feral birds behave badly.
Obnoxious delinquents
betray royal lineage.

Halloween on Kauai

Tropical trees spill candy corn blooms.
Hawaiian spiders weave timely webs,
snare rainbow sun beams falling through limbs.

Ghosts and tombstones pop out
from between bougainvillea, anthurium, orchids.
Jack-o-lanterns have collapsed in the heat.

Rooster descendants screech at red sunrise.
Spirits of Kauai royalty linger along coral reefs,
among Napali canyons, volcanic stones.

Hanalei Halloween

All Hallow's Eve on Kauai--women in cat's ears and whiskers,
a haram girl's outfit, pool boys dressed like the devil.

A Grateful Dead skeleton riffs beneath red bandanna.
His stage—a carved pumpkin perched upon a faux cow skull.

Bat wings stretch, poised for Halloween flight
within scarlet scarab.
Love beads wrap the base of a gravestone protruding from turban.

Candy corn, bed sheet ghosts, eight-legged plastic spiders.
I take refuge on the lanai, treat myself to a mai tai.

Tahiti Nui

Halloween artifacts dangle above the bar, shelves of booze;
cobwebs and plastic spiders drape bamboo rafters.

Heat and humidity seduce locals seeking cold beer.
Tables of rowdy tourists knock back famous mai tais.

A leftover barfly solicits handouts on the front porch
as a lethargic barrista scrubs down faded counters.

Live Hawaiian Music Every Night a sad poster announces.
I watch our pregnant waitress step around sleeping roosters,

admire this laid-back lifestyle of the northern shore
where everyone moves at the speed of slow drying paint.

I imagine Gauguin and his buxom babes on a tropical beach,
naked skin baked to hues of molasses, cinnamon, honey.

Bubba Burgers

I head north, cross a one lane bridge,
descend to taro fields, kudzu,
philodendron smothered palms,
make my annual pilgrimage
for greasy beef at Bubba Burgers.

Roosters and mourning doves
queue up for fried crumbs
dropped by diners at outdoor tables.
I munch and swallow succulent poison,
observe taut Hanalei surfers, sleek wahines,
feel fat cells multiply, arteries harden.

Molten

Pele stirs, kindles volcanic ridge line.
Clouds flush, simmer ominously.
Above gilded ocean, pulsing celestial embers.

Storm front rolls ashore, buffets green headlands.
Morning light liquefies, saturated with water.
Demoralized roosters – sodden, bedraggled.

Clingy humidity embraces on contact.
Showers steam against bare skin,
batters bougainvillea, plumeria blossoms.

Rooster Reveille

I wake to rain, distant roar
of gargantuan surf.

Daybreak oozes dim silver
across red lava ridge line.

From beneath wind-battered ginger,
the relay chorus begins.

Up and down the ragged shore,
scarlet roosters screech in unison.

Pele's draggled children cock-a-doodle-doo
their complaints from beneath sodden ti leaves.

After Deluge

Palm fronds bat morning air like wings of ascending green angels.
Bright sunrise lifts lavender lids, delivers clear morning.

Scent of vanilla macadamia coffee drifts from the kitchen
where I spread strawberry preserves over a muffin.

Rain storms have passed after stripping trees of their blossoms.
Mist lifts, reveals hills, the cabin-fevered outside and walking.

Tiny lizards skitter across steaming cement, disappear under ginger.
Geese and roosters patrol sodden lawns, forage for breakfast.

I scribble, unable to capture what spirits are saying.
consider tossing in the towel, regrouping poolside.

From Westin to St. Regis

Along the hiking trail
above Hanalei Bay,
pink blossoms cascade
from frangipani.

Tiny egrets scatter
as I huff uphill,
a red, sweaty tourist
unaccustomed to heat.

Morning sun blares, etches
puffy cumulous on a purple horizon.
Everywhere, the crooning of invisible doves,
pervasive scent of gardenias.

Lazy waves cream luxuriously
against submerged coral,
unroll foamy surf, an invitation
to disappear upon hidden beaches.

Princeville Meander

Mist mingles with passing clouds,
drapes wrinkled Na Pali ridge line.
I huff through humidity, heat,
scatter roosters, hens, baby chicks.
Invisible doves croon from fragrant
groves of tiny gardenias.

On the golf course, a man circles the greens,
steers a bright yellow mower trailing a wake
of fluttering, foraging egrets.
Joggers thunder past, offer "Good morning!"
I wind through eucalyptus, pause to admire
bracts of lavender orchids, scarlet hibiscus.

Today there is nothing important on my agenda.
I can choose among scribbling, reading, a leisurely swim.
Settle for contented contemplation of turquoise surf,
white capped reefs, sip a passionfruit mimosa on my veranda.

Hanalei Overlook

Seething clouds mimic smoke from a mythical dragon.
I park illegally, contemplate patchwork fields, banana tree valley.
Palms and kudzu vines dominate riverbanks,
below, taro fields and sugar cane intersected by ginger.

Observing local custom, we take turns
crossing a one lane bridge above turgid water.
At the Dolphin Cafe, diners sip umbrella drinks,
entertained by kayakers as they wait for sashimi.

Silvery Hanalei Bay glitters with paddle boarders and surfers.
Overhead, soggy cumulus contuse, spill lukewarm sprinkles.
At road's end, a vendor hawks shave ice near eroded caves,
where a muddy trail marks taboo bones of ancient royalty.

Kauai Rain

Palm trees battered by rain perform a frenzied hula.
Storm winds roil ocean, raise gigantic breakers.
Sodden roosters hunker in ginger plant thickets.
Mist steams from pastures, erases overgrown hillsides.

Protected and dry in my third story condo,
I sip macadamia coffee, scribble poetry, spin TV channels.
Spy upon laughing couples within a small hot tub.
Admire gyrating banana trees, dripping cabanas.

Taro

"I don't know where such certainty comes from – the brave flesh or the theater of the mind..." – Mary Oliver

Rain clouds simmer
across blue Sleeping Giant,
disintegrate above taro quilts,
feathery palms, curlicue river.

Green undulates downhill
to pulsing, cerulean ocean.
Along muddy gully
descending to coral beach,
roosters chase mourning doves
into pink ginger.

I ponder ragged Kalalea peak,
imagine fire gods whose burning hands
shaped this red island.
Their bones decompose under
blossoming mountain.

Calavera for Kauai

The ancients speak through Pele's children,
scarlet roosters who reprimand pushy Nene geese,
chase tiny mourning doves into hibiscus.

Steep Na Pali coastline hides royal bones.
The jagged silhouette of a sleeping giant
lifts volcanic hills, sprouts ghostly plumeria.

Kauai sneezes silver rain,
scatters battalions of wandering banyan.
Poetry spills from belligerent clouds.

Tree Tunnel

Twin rows of gnarled shade trees
frame volcanic trail.
White egrets frisk damp meadow
as roosters and their harems
scratch for grubs.
Tiny mourning doves croon.

Bronze sunrise lasers
above streaked ocean,
fluffy clouds.
Along the Na Pali ridge,
a sleeping giant
juts his green silhouette
from philodendron thickets,
plumeria groves.

I wander Princeville's perimeter,
admire red ginger, pink hibiscus,
stop to pet passing dogs,
cling to comfortable shade.

Approaching the Day of the Dead

Hard rain slants inland,
spews purple payload
into navy blue ocean.
Draggled roosters crow,
raise what passes for light.
We wake, move together,
celebrate thirteen years
as soul-mates and lovers.

Palm trees whisper secrets,
how to survive tropical storms,
endure by being flexible,
willing to bend.
Below our bedroom,
a nagging Nene goose honks,
chases her beleaguered partner
across sodden grass.

After breakfast burritos,
we share guava mimosas,
toast companionship,
its ups and downs,
laugh at demonic jack o-lanterns
scattered among scarlet ti,
mark another anniversary
on the Day of the Dead.

Hanalei Bay Resort

Daylight's last gasp
flares over Bali Hai,
lasers gold across Hanalei Bay
where an anchored sailboat
sways above lazy sets
of incoming waves.

Surfers reluctant
to return to shore,
paddle, push upright
to take their final ride
onto waiting white beach.

Coconut palms hula
in balmy evening breeze.
Bright stars, thin crescent
of waning moon,
glow against navy sky.

Plumeria

Perfume and crooning doves
start a clear day.

I wander rough trail,
circumvent golf course
above fern fringed cliffs,
hike to sparkling beach.

Tiny violet orchids
spill from moist clefts
in immense, knotted trees.
Waxy plumeria blooms,
tropical winter's inside joke,
festoon denuded limbs.

I inhale erotic, exotic essence,
nearly swoon
from pleasurable scent.

Sunset on Kauai

Clouds spill their storm over ocean.
Roosters and their drab paramours frisk wet lawn,
dissect sodden ginger roots, excavate dinner.

Empty cumulus sail between lanky palms,
glow pink, then peach as sunlight vanishes.
White surf rolls over coral; gray horizon turns purple.

Invisible doves croon from thickening shadow.
A flash of starlight, flit of wing.
Warm night whispers tropical secrets.

I sip a glass of wine,
inhale trade wind perfume,
serene in this lavender moment.

Cancun

Half-hearted rain clouds
float above placid ocean.
We rise, shower, settle on balcony
with plates of fresh, tropical fruit,
sip gigantic lattes.

Below us, fan palms undulate.
Invisible, exotic birds chatter.
Early risers slide into infinity pool.
We lethargically plan what to explore
as humidity rises.

Poetry knocks on the soul's door,
infiltrates bright, breezy moment.
Even tough iguanas within broken
temple ruins feel the urge to emerge,
share resplendent sunshine, resonant musings.

Tulum (2018)

Mayan spirits lurk
within crypts to avoid
gringo touristas.

Vendors hawk scarlet
horned diablo masks
for a few pesos.

Battered stone cairns
under fleeting storm clouds spill
chain-mailed iguanas.

Iguana

Drab watchdog of ancient Mayan ruins
reclines upon rock wall, nearly invisible
beneath banyan shadows.

He barely turns fringed skull,
obsidian eyes, to oversee
my slow, precarious passage.

Indigenous tribes are no more,
replaced by tourists, modern hotels.
Jagged stones remain, frame cluttered skyline.

Macaws

In Xel-Ha, captive dolphins,
caged manatees
exist in watery corrals
where they swim
among paying tourists.

I ride downriver
on a plastic inner tube.
Once ashore, I catch my breath,
sip a virgin pina colada.
Shrieking teens splash land
in pristine lagoons
from slippery zip lines.

To my left, branches filled with
colorful indigenous parrots
chatter, unfurl crimson wings,
offer avian comments.

A visitor defies posted rules,
proffers a tidbit.
This ignites a barrage
of squawks, disgruntled flapping
among the unfed.
Park staff coerce offenders onto sticks,
haul them off for a time-out.

Later, sunburnt and exhausted,
I pose with a brilliant macaw
atop my head, wonder
how carelessly we appropriate nature
for our thoughtless amusement.

Lifeguard

Pillows of pale cumulus
balloon overhead.
I share a swimming pool
with long-legged blackbird.
He watches me sidestroke
through tepid water,
lap after lap.

By 9 a.m., sunburnt tourists
at the swim up bar
drink Bloody Mary's
I swill poetry,
scribble stories.

Wind rises,
ruffles yellowing palm trees
offers early warning
to bellwether changes
coming my way.

Yucatan Menage

Frigate birds and parasailing tourists
spiral above three shades of turquoise surf,
a blinding white beach.

We trudge through uncertain waves,
ignore whistling shore-side peddlers who hawk hats,
corn row weaves, candid photos of drunks.

Mornings, I putter among Mayan ruins,
hunt elusive iguanas between ancient stones,
sip hot coffee high above an infinite horizon pool.

Nights, I guzzle margaritas,
scribble to describe exotic adventures
that unfold as vacation days pass.

In dream, I immigrate from stress,
find a quiet oasis where I fit
in some magical realm.

Isla Mujeres

An over-the-hill mariachi singer,
minus his band,
entertains sunburnt tourists
clustered topside
on a blue and gold ferry.
He warbles, clogs,
proffers plastic tip jug,
collects a few pesos.

I disembark,
wander down the cracked sidewalk,
acid orange soda in hand,
to sign a contract,
hand over driver's license,
retrieve rickety golf cart.

Bumping along a narrow street,
I admire pink, gold, turquoise
taquerias, bars, private casas.
Hitting speed bumps too fast,
I give myself whiplash.
Iguanas glare from beneath
bougainvillea tangles.

Stopping at a quaint café,
I sit upon glistening beach,
sip a pina colada,
munch lobster tacos.
Yucatan sun bakes away
every worry.

Tulum (2012)

Iguanas in all sizes waddle from limestone ruins,
stunted palms, up skinny steps to broken temples.

We squeeze our large, American bodies
through ancient gates, tiny stone tunnels.

Mayan gods in blurry relief decorate fading walls,
falling facades, having outlived their original sculptors.

A shattered tower still overlooks dark cliffs,
slanting trees, Caribbean breakers.

Rainclouds bubble toward open seas.
We wander and wonder.

Chubby tourists now shriek and frolic
where warriors once unloaded their canoes.

Cameras and tour guides capture only hints
of an overthrown culture.

Acknowledgements

The author is grateful to the editors of the following publications for originally publishing her work.

"Bronze Stud," "Paris at Midnight," "Pere Lachaise," *Dead Snakes,* July 10, 2014.

"Love Among Ruin," "Heloise's Epistle," & "Notre Dame Symphony," *Dead Snakes*, March 3, 2015.

"Montemarte Adventure," "Cabaret After Sunrise," & "Strike," *Dead Snakes,* March 14, 2015.

"Persistent Memory," "Visiting Versailles," *Dead Snakes,* March 20, 2015.

"Expatriate," "Carne," & "Mimo," *Dead Snakes,* April 24, 2015.

"Madrid," "Alicante Beach Esplanade," & "Tapas y Tequila," *Dead Snakes,* May 5, 2015.

"Pim Pam Pollo," *Yellow Chair Review*, Issue 3, 2015.

"Autumn on Kauai," *Silver Birch Press (My Perfect Vacation Series).*

"Princeville Sunrise," "Sunset on Kauai," "Hanalei Overlook," *Conceit Magazine.*

"Trade Winds," "Bubba Burgers," "Molten," "After Deluge," *Dead Snakes.*

"Halloween on Kauai," *Nomad's Choir.*

"Plumeria," *Naturewriting.com.*

About the Author

Jennifer Lagier lives a block from the Monterey stage where Janis Joplin performed and Jimi Hendrix torched his guitar. She served as Area Coordinator and instructor with California Poets in the Schools, taught at Modesto Junior College, California State University Monterey Bay, Hartnell College and Monterey Peninsula College. Jennifer has published twenty books and has work appearing in a variety of anthologies and literary magazines. Blue Light Press published her full-length poetry collections *Harbingers* and *Meditations on Seascapes and Cypress*. Her forthcoming book, *Weeping in the Promised Land* will be published in Fall 2023 by Kelsay Books. A former editor for the *Homestead Review*, she now edits the *Monterey Poetry Review* and helps coordinate Monterey Bay Poetry Consortium Second Saturday readings.

Website: jlagier.net, Facebook: www.facebook.com/JenniferLagier/

www.ingramcontent.com/pod-product-compliance
Lightning Source LLC
Chambersburg PA
CBHW031203160426
43193CB00008B/488